Difficult Gifts

Publication © Modjaji Books 2011
Text © Dawn Garisch 2011

First published in 2011 by Modjaji Books PTY Ltd
P O Box 385, Athlone, 7760, South Africa
modjaji.books@gmail.com
http://modjaji.book.co.za

ISBN: 978-1-920397-32-6

Book and cover design: Natascha Mostert
Cover artwork: Katherine Glenday
Editor: Fiona Zerbst
Printed and bound by Mega Digital, Cape Town
Set in Georgia

Difficult Gifts

Poems by Dawn Garisch

modjaji books

Contents

The Edge

Standing top heavy at the back door
of my childhood home,
holding fast to the edge
of the low wall, my ankles unstable,
my heart surging, turbulent . . .

Fred, the cook, head level
with mine as he crouches, anchored
to the earth, throws out lines to help me
over. His fez beckons red as a beacon.

I let myself loose, launch myself out
on my maiden voyage, glee
gusting my body across
the impossible, and into his arms.

Great Fish

My father caught great fish, tiger fish.
He pulled their gleaming, dancing bodies
from the jaws of the Zambezi, severed
and salted their heads and strung them up to dry:
necklaces of death.

I felt them watching as I played
with trucks, earth and sticks,
amongst the mielie stalks;
their trapped, flat eyes
never leaving my back.

Sometimes I would chance a look
and see their rows of razor teeth
invite the blood that leapt in my finger
to touch them.

I could have touched,
seen my blood run.

I went inside at my mother's call,
washed the dirt off my hands and face,
sat still and straight at a white, starched table,
and ate their bodies.

Elephant Park

Heavy in me. The grey weight bearing
down, the slow certain sturdy gait
that stops and waits. Patient. Well trained.
We regard each other over rails
and stakes. The ranger says: now
we can stretch our palms out, offer chunks
of fruit to the sensitive ancient trunks
and mouths. No sudden movements. Now
they are allowed out and we stand
beside them. We pose, our tentative hands
against the immense tired silent flanks
while they pick at pellets that nourish, tame.
We smile as cameras snap and flash
to catch us in the act: power
staged and trained, straining.

Do we remember?
Remember the awe and terror.
Without us, these giants would die.
Without us, they would flourish.

Dawn Garisch

The Proper Use Of Flowers

I fall in love with men
who bring me flowers
picked from my own garden:

tossed salad bouquets
on fragrant platters
threaded vines all hung about like lights.

They stand expectant at my threshold
and point out things I've never noticed:

switchblade blooms that pierce the air with colour
brass ensembles setting fire to music.

My mother had a garden once
all hemmed about with jagged brick.
I remember fitting foxgloves on my fingers:
a floral witch!
but then was scolded
and taught the proper use of flowers.

Now I sit, the books discarded,
worm my fingers into the earth's secret place
take root
and wait:
for those that come and show me to myself.

The Elements

He wrestles with the elements
to make a good braai.

She, in the kitchen,
finds a green worm

on a lettuce leaf
and trying to keep rational
flushes it down the toilet.

Nowadays, he showers alone,
closes the glass sliding doors.
Stands encased in glass, imagines
he is in the middle of a thunderstorm.

She walks in the garden, design in her mind,
a shopping list for the nursery.

In bed, she lets him cover her
like a cloud, and is surprised each time
by feelings she doesn't understand.

Making Fire

To make fire, they say you need
a shaft of soft wood directed
in a notch in hard wood
then rotated fast until the tip begins to smoke
and loosen. In pairs the work is lessened
but involves another kind of learning.

Do not hasten.
Heat takes time to take and grow.
Observe the fruit: embers, red as fallen apples,
drop to the catch of a metal tray.

Again, take time, be kind. If failing, try again.
An ember lives long enough to be transferred
and buried in a clutch of kindling.

Patience, now. Long, slow bellows of breath
encourage combustion and the loosening of light
out of the heart of matter,
the luminous released and falling upwards into air.

We made fire, you and I,
our intentions bent over this common task,
our movements starting shy and faulty,
trying to align ourselves to work the rhythm
of this meeting of heart and matter,

trying to catch the febrile spark
before it either faltered or fell to ruinous burning.

At times your face shows signs of a man
who's been burnt; it's in your eyes, that searing.
In cupped hands I guard a tiny flame that almost died
when I gave it to another's keeping.

How will we make hearth warmth together,
while trying to align these singed wounds, these brands and cinders?

Patience; let us tend the ember,
slowly stoking a gentle combustion
to loosen despair from the heart of matter,
the numinous released and falling upwards into air.

Every man

Every man is possible.
Possibly a door leading to a secret garden.
Every man has a handle, hidden.
Men are locked, even to themselves.
Mysteriously, the key has vanished.

I crouch down, put my pupil to the keyhole.
The open door of me bangs impatiently
in the wind. We're lost, on all fours,
searching, banging heads.

We imagine we are looking for the same thing.

I find something green, shaped
like a keyhole. A keyhole is not
complete without a key. As a woman,
I cannot insert myself.

I imagine the garden perfect, doused
in light. It grows and lives without me, impossibly perfect
without me.

Cheesemaker

It was what he did with ease
with milk – suckling the lush mother liquid
from a goat's teat with strong strokes
of his fingers, the bucket filling white –

the yield of soil delivered
into this simple twist:
grass to milk, milk to cheese,
the slow curds encouraged:

cut, warmed, salted, compressed;

then aged until the day
a slivered sacrament
passes my lips.

Bee Man

The man I met with kind, hurt eyes,
– over drinks at a braai –
described his work with bees:
how he'd hold a swarm,
drunk with smoke, in his arms.
I could see it: armfuls of sleepy bees
pouring from his embrace – slow honey.

He put a glass of mead he'd made
into my hand. The smooth honey-wine
slid into my centre and stung.
I wanted more

but as day succumbed to night,
with the insistent buzzing of insects,
I saw how he undid himself
– smoking drunk –
unable to hold a thing except
the ferment trapped inside his face –
swollen and red
with the woken rage of bees.

Difficult Gifts

Two Gifts

I've lived in my body in this city all my life
yet have not known this simple pleasure:
you took me to a lake on a fynbos berg.
I entered like a dream, plunging.

We sat on white sand playing
with shoals of meaning that shift
when you lift the lid off words.
You chose to sit alone while I went in.

The mountain offers up this cup
for gulls and clouds to drink;
I baptised my life within its living liquid,
emerging blessed. I heard you say

women want more than you can give; a man
was drowning in your eye. We walked back,
caressed by sensuous air. Your mouth
was tense. I shook your hand goodbye.

Landslide

This time of opening;
this hut cambered to the mountain's wide shrug.
You – your hand in the crevice of my womanhood –
rock climber, brought to your knees.

Outside, the wind puzzles round a flagstaff,
frogs cry out for love across the night.
Torrents tumble down abraded slopes
of mountain rubble released in the flood's wake.

Inside, our blood rises.
You scour my skin open,
my heart spread like a map
for your ascent.

I am plumbed – my heart rends
like a tent door to admit you. The moon
arrives, the shade of an owl flits by.
We sleep fitfully, on sated, unstable earth.

Leiwater

Despite the solid pegs of olive trees,
land escapes in strokes of brittle brush
and dust towards infinity; I want to enter,
but a sallow heat has soaked the shade
and shallow bedrock is a barricade.

Wednesdays arrive; we rise to meet
with our appointed hour, to switch
the sluice gates in the ditch;
we watch as channelled water flows and floods
and penetrates the land to mud. It's then

I bar the door and lead you to my body
long held shy and parched these years,
when I escaped to hide inside the shadow
of burnt stone. It is an act of grace:
those times when I arrive beside you,

despite the years my earth was scorched
and I believed that rain and green
would never come again.
We are anointed in this place; receive
abundance in an arid land.

Switzerland

Everywhere I ride
hunched astride this metal frame
delighting in the bite of gears
surging beside fields of brushed wheat:
stroked, matt-golden, flecked with poppy red,
where sunflowers lift their childlike heads;

everywhere I ride
trundling the macadam under or
whizzing down a winding forest pass
leaning my wellbeing on a wedge of solid air
meandering near a chivvying mountain stream
descending to the shuffling edge, the languid laze of lake,

everywhere I ride
through towns of houses packed tight against the coming cold
windows with their vivid shutter wings pinned open
sprout coloured flowers that sing and urge against the grey
fountains on the corners spout soliloquies on life
venerable decaying walls give root to plants
redolence of dung hangs on the heavy summer air

everywhere I ride
- my body reeling curious through this world -
everywhere I carry you inside, inside me,
cradled in the hidden sling of my lilting, venturous heart.

Another North

I am turning from you
my body swivelling magnetic to another north.

I'm turning to the constant pull
that once wore your countenance,
turning away from the bay of you
nosing out into seas ploughed by storms
I'm sailing into drowning
with a packet of kissed earth stitched to my naked hip
threaded through my bone.

Portrait of a Marriage

Between the years the layers
between the layers of years you entered
my life a tree of spring leaves
you drew me to you through you
taught me how to enter love how to love you.

Between the soft leaves of my sex unfolding you slid
the leaves of my heart valves skipping their beats
between the beat and spurt and slipstream of bloodties
my bloodknot untied and spliced to your life
through your side I sighed
my form unfolding origami
resolving to be true, true to this story
unfolding new as green leaves.

Between the sheets, scenes and stages
I entered with you, you taught me
to love your body my body
to lay my body down my life
blind inspired I slid inside our story
the babies, timetables and weary nights.
You taught me to believe
you would not leave me bereaved
between the sheets between the beds we made
beds of spinach and leavened loaves rising
the laundered clothes the mealtime tables
the years of our loving, and hating.

Between the spring and autumn of it all
you taught me to taper myself
my very foot root caught in the boulder of you
between loud stones the silent fissure of you
holding what was true
what I thought was true
you taught me to be patient, tenacious
curious and kind
your acts of kindness left me
mindful and grateful.

Between promises and what transpired
between your random acts of kindness to others
between your other lovers
you left me
autumn layered leaves.

Between intentions and your crimes of desire
you taught me about loss, how leaves
ungreen, burn and drop,
unlearn lessons of spring receiving
seasons turn, trees unseam.

Between layers of believing and despair
your absence taught me that writing retrieves me
retrieves scattered debris laid out
like death a poem a prophesy
my pen raking shattered words
new words seeding
sown into leaves this leaving
these shedding trees laying down their lives
for me for my life tree
paper reams sheaves of paper
taught me how to lay my life down
how to enter these book-marks and earth-works.

Between lines inscribed because of you
you taught me to unbind my life my love
to untwine my root from you
you taught me the difference between loving and lies
between the bed and the door
both made of trees laying down their lives
between seeing my life through your eyes
or through mine
you taught me not to believe your story about me
not to believe you to leave you
between these acts that line my life you taught me
not to love you
to leave you
you taught me how to leave.

Home

bit my hand last night;
the door released me from its jaw
then skulked away, leaving me
to dance upon a bright hot
coin of pain.

Dog Days

1.
As a child I was told to be nice
to dogs I did not like.
My hand would puppet out to greet them:
hot hair, hard wound bodies,
my compliant smile pulled tight,
as they nudged me with their muzzles.

2.
A passing stranger told me once
on the pavement outside my house
that his dog would not have bitten me
if I were a nicer girl.

3.
Years ago across a room a lover snarled at me
that his cocker spaniel loved him more
than I would ever do.

4.
You cringe, so sorry,
so sorry for yourself.
A dead dog lies between us.

5.
Bounding loose and open-limbed,
dogs don't seem to realise
their petty lives are circumscribed
by the grating tin-opener,
the lasso of the whistle.

6.
I lie awake
stapled to the face of night
by dogbark.

7.
A bone is all you offer.
I no longer come
when you call.

Drowning

The Chief Engineer is a handsome man.
He knows what it takes to make a ship
go. He controls
controls the engine.
He caresses the casings.
Like a farmer far from help
he makes a plan.

At night we sleep
we sleep safe in our bunks.
The Chief Engineer and the Captain,
they know
they know where they're going.

He leans forward slightly
whenever I speak.
The engine noise
noise during all the years
has damaged his reception.

The Chief Engineer has a land life
too: a fourbyfour,
a country house, a wife,
a wife and a Staffordshire puppy.

He buys me a drink
the night before
before we dock, tells me
about his hernia op,
that cock size doesn't matter.

Also: that he loves
he loves his wife.
I see it coming:
he'll offer me a life
a lifeboat meanwhile
meanwhile this man is drowning.

The Chief Engineer says he might need Viagra
or not. I am, after all, the ship's doctor
and know what it takes
to make a man
to make a man go.

Carefully I explain
explain I'm divorcing a man
who dropped anchor
into a number
a number of women.

The Chief Engineer sails
he sails straight ahead,
he hasn't heard any
anything, offers me pleasure,
pleasure in exchange
in exchange for:
pleasure.

I laugh
laugh without laughter
go alone to my bunk
and cannot sleep cannot
sleep because of my dream:

my dream of the Chief Engineer trying
to hoist his limp sail trying
to navigate his life trying

while out
in the bay out
of earshot
drowns his beautiful wife.

Into The Valley

The highway I assumed my whole life ends here.
Into wilderness I descend,
following the river that saws its way
through stone, going somewhere, deeper, nowhere;

staying here. Trying to find the thread, or thing
I need to look for. Mountains, cut with tracts
of stone, rise on either side. They shatter
slowly, feeding fragments into flow.

The renovated farmhouse has lost its hearth.
I fumble with gas and matches, making tea,
my last solace, trying to trace the question
your hand left on my breast. Outside,

the amphitheatre stands – broken rocks
arranged into a stony stare. They frown
against my complaint, watching. My teeth
crush a rusk; these grindstones won't last.

Down by the stream a toppled rock provides
the sun to lie on, but the ozone layer
is lost, and my sons are leaving, leaving
with their lives. There is no soft word for stone.

These rocks observe my passing with indifferent
grey. Boulders angle from the earth
like whales breaching, or ships going down.
I'm filled with atrophy, the yield of youth gone.

The mountain shrugs its mottled shoulders,
shedding stone. Boulders spill from hill crown,
rearranged by water and the tug of earth,
slow to find their way in the long dance down.

Sliced rocks accost the skyline, finger clouds
or penetrate the earth. Or wait, unmoved.
Don't they know there is a time for brimstone?
The thrown moon falls. Nights wander without sleep.

This edge of rock against the sky,
these lines of ants and insect tracks, reveal
a coded tiding unlike any other language.
All words on which I rest my case are lost,

stumbling in the dead end of my mind.
Annotated in still rock is the fable
of restless river, playful tale of wind.
The massif reveals its tip; below, its dark bulk

lies trapped, hibernating in the sand.
Here, the armadillo stones root, squat.
They note my long descent, scornful,
malevolent. My life is water in my hand.

The sun-struck rock is rutted and cracked
like elephant. Boulders lean and mourn,
or copulate, or fist their silent faces to
the sky, or lock against each other, waiting

for the earth to shift. Here, within the slow
refrain of stone, is water, plaited round
a rock, and turquoise-faced iguana
performing press-ups, insects digesting

in the sticky leaves of plants. I stand apart;
for when my heart stops, I cannot feed the earth
that fed me. I place a pebble on my tongue, another
in my sex, to weigh me down to this soil,

to weight me with this ground.

Difficult Gifts

Slow dozing

Slow dozing in bed,
releasing thoughts of you:
how it could have been
and how it is instead.

Bluebeard's gift

Tonight I saw right through
the keyhole of your pupil,
into my darkest room.

I am burnt by my own spotlight;
I hang from the meat hook
of my own butchery.

Here there are no prizes,
no keys.

To the Sisters

who keep vigil in the light-drained hours
strung like a rosary: hail mary full of grace

you were with me, blessed was I
amongst women as I waited

alone for my firstborn to tear from my body,
my milk white in the vast dark of his night;

alone for my bruised and fallen son
to choose, nailed between death and life;

alone and home, sick with waiting,
his grasp as slender as the reed of his throat;

alone while other women raise elated faces
to men, then fall back empty, waiting

alone at home with their tender sons while men
rise to penetrate the night – and walk away.

Appointment

The waiting room contains several people, waiting. Those who can read flip through magazines; others stare at the wall inside their faces, their white sticks tucked at their sides. They come, like me, waiting in their skins, waiting for hope, cure and light.

The world is fading.

Inside my eye I embark
on a trampoline parabola,
grappling weightlessness against gravity.
Up here, I can see beyond the wall, I can see
through catches in conversation, past
the incomplete gesture, I catch
the bat-flit across a face. I look
for an answer.

The receptionist calls. I stare bereft at the ophthalmologist's stab of light, consumed by the need to puncture night. He leans back, head erased by blur. On the wall behind him hangs a box of lit letters that have nothing to do with love or story.

After-images bloom in darkness;
film burns open, fades to black
thumbs press prints down hard
inside my tired eyes.

The doctor says, sincerely: The important difference is between dark and light.

Images fall through holes,
through blanks in absence.

I leave clutching another important appointment. I can barely see through tears as I walk away, fettered by images of flight.

The Owls

We live next door to graves and owls;
some avert their eyes to say
we flirt with night, and brush
too close to that we should not touch.
But earth is lined with death
and we are rooted in it,
the dirt of us already packed
black beneath some future farmer's
fingernails; buried bones
lie karossed in wood and fleece
dead blood seeps through soil
in long red ochre entrails.

Eyelashes fall, dissipate into sleep.

The owls preside,
pegged upon two fence posts;
they linger, rotate their heads
and arc their eyes in vigilance.
On the ground they've posted pellets
of rodent bones and fur; the tree above
roots down and stirs ancestral wrists and ribs.

A wind sweeps past, alive
with millions of last, expelled breaths.
Dust settles softly on our table.
We sit and eat, drink and talk till late
and arc our eyes.
Silently we survey the dark.

Like owls, we sit and wait.

To My Father, Who Died

On shimmering beaches you come to me
and sit in the caves of my sockets,
taking a long look across the wash
to where the sea breathes white and ash,

seasoned with fish and salt.
You are oblivious to views, cliffs
and gulls in flight, unless they relate
to where to cast, where to meditate.

Your eyes skim and skip, scanning
the churned water, the lure within,
wanting to plunge into the rip
where fish disperse like coins in light.

Your sperm immersed, scattered,
pearled inside my mother's cavern,
fastened on her blood muscle
some limpet days; then the third daughter,

sea child, washed up like diviner's shells
and other flotsam drifting to your shores,
fine lines cast by receding tides
upon your palms, now ash to the wind.

That place, that interface where fish emerge
you have entered. I sit a while and watch
the surface play and try to understand
what moved you. I see only the view.

A Necessary Tearing

This time of opening; in the bedroom
your husband pools the yellow of his liver
in his slack skin and turns his eyes inward
to the place we cannot see. Outside

the swimming pool grows green with leaves,
the pump arrested. Above, the tree's arms
hold out a few remaining flaming flags.
There is a necessary tearing here

as the soul departs – a rent that opens
the known world, allowing the impossible
to enter. The wind subsides; his breathing rests.
The tree stands naked right throughout the winter

its fingers sifting through the shifting sky.
The doctor closes David's empty eyes.
His last breath lies easy now.
In time, the rift will seal.

Hogsback

Immersed in green leaf-filtered light,
this shaded air, this branched and
brambled valley where trees feed
on their own dead fallen leaves, and
the stream ambles over rocks towards
the distant sea, where the mist breathes
a white and silent poultice on the glade,
and the sky slides easily over serrated
canopies, I notice, at last, my persistent
grief disperse and fade.

The Weakest Link

I wonder what will pack up first:
my liver or my knees?
In old age, what will come off worst:
My ears or coronaries?

What might remain to use again:
my kidneys or my eyes?
Which body part will halt my brain -
the cause of my demise?

Which organ is my weakest link
which one will stop my breath?
 A lung collapse, a colon kink -
the aperture for Death.

Saviour

The shepherd chases off the wolf
and soothes the lamb's wild bleating.
He knows that in a week or two
the lamb will be good eating.

Fated

He was a mole
trapped below asphalt. She
was a fly who mistook glass
for sky. They would've got on,
having things in common; yet,
they never met.

The Manual of Common Sense: Chapter 249

Behind each man who cheats his wife,
is a woman who comes to assist him.
She doesn't slow down to check on his life;
It would seem she cannot resist him.

"Oh, love me sweet, please honour me true!"
With her body she tries to enlist him.
Now why suppose he'll be different with you?
True lies have a way of persisting.

Over the wall

They've bricked the garden round the pool
to solve the moles, the chore of grass,
the unpredictability of insects.
Baked bricks ice the earth,
enough to build a small church.

On Saturday nights
my neighbour's friends
occupy this horizontal wall
 they've found their niche –
laugh and braai, smoke and sing
karaoke; drink and splash and sink.

The Anatomy of Poetry

It seems my heart is not a pump,
nor gristly fist that's primed to clutch
and clench and thereby force
my life blood forward.

A thoughtful surgeon found this poem –
he unpicked the heart's impeccable stitch
along its seam, and found that it's
a twisted rope – double-twisted –
looped and helixed back upon itself.

He stopped to note the knotted heart's
faithful labour, and saw: it wrings blood out,
cup by careful cupful – more akin to washing
day, than to that of fitted factory parts.

The anatomy of poetry is often lost
within the eye's design. And at such cost.

Blood Delta

Last night at dinner around a white linen table,
deep magenta wine held ellipsed in the spill
of light after years of ripening in silence,
a man I know plunged his fork into his lamb
well-marinaded, slow-oven-cooked, and said
he admired Nigeria for hanging Ken Saro Wiwa.
The gravy ran, oil fields spilt their slick. I went home,

and wept for words that have never left my lips
nor fingers. I did not object. My heart kept fisting
my unspilt blood round and round. What use
these hacked marks and scribbles, these clasps
of sound. A frightened man who wields the fork
of power will not be swayed by talk or inky dribbles.

Saro Wiwa said it did not matter if he lived or died,
but that we try to make the world a better place.
Will his blood courage purge the Niger Delta?
What word can change the river of the world?

History

As a child I pictured the history of Africa:
Dingaan betraying Piet Retief
at dinner. Today in my son's textbook
I see how a black man sits
and looks sits and looks
at two objects lying at his feet.
You can tell by the hunch
of his shoulders, by the way his hands hang
slack; you can tell by the faces
of the other black men standing round, helpless –
look at him: look: look this man failed,
failed to obtain his quota
on a Congolese rubber plantation. Therefore,
therefore and forever,
he sits and looks sits and looks
at the severed hands of his five-year-old daughter.

She said she'd had a normal childhood

On Sundays, after lunch, her father took time out from work.
He'd rest until the heat drained away, and the shadows
bled their lengths along the front lawn to merge
with twilight.

All paths converged on her childhood home with the clinic
at the back. Those who came on Sunday afternoons looking
for the doctor, would sit on a bench in the kitchen
and wait.

The district surgeon's daughter, assisted by the maid, would clean
their gaping scalps. The smell of roast mingled with the odour
of blood and cheap wine breath. She'd dab, align, dab
and stitch.

No anaesthetic, yet they didn't flinch while she worked above
their bent heads. With basic needlework techniques learnt at school
she closed them back into their skins. They were the lucky ones,
she said.

Mondays, early, the police would offload those whose wounds
had gone too deep. The long, bled bodies lay upon the front lawn
awaiting autopsy. Her friends on their way to school would slow down,
and gape.

Love Imagined

When my firstborn turned eighteen
I gave him a rucksack
and imagined him into the world
without me.

He thanked me, absent-
mindedly, already gone.

Lament is the sound I can make in a car
when I drive alone.

My friend took me in,
unbound my clothes from my body,
ran a shower and stood me there to feel
my hot loss leaving me.

She scrubbed my skin
as though I were a horse she loved,
then towelled my heaving body, even between my toes,
between my legs she patted me dry.

She fetched the oil of sesame
and soothed it into me, anointing
even my ear lobes,
my elbows,

then she closed my eyes
with a fold of cloth, and slowly,
very slowly,
she fed me something sweet and nut
like nougat
to help me imagine myself back
into the world
without him.

On being a single mother living with two adolescent sons

Our house is full of the trials of Eros:
Cornered telephones and sedentary poses;
Walls lean, dissolving; doors slam closed.

Lyrics arrive in the middle of breakfast;
The air thickens with a fog of burnt toast.
Car keys are lost beneath an avalanche of lust.

A lit candle floats in the eye's glass bowl.
Dawn stumbles over restless night's threshold.
The spread of unencumbered bed turns cold.

From space this house is a normal home;
The moon's long arm enters every room,
Fingering eyelids open into catacombs.

Women swimming

Two women swimming in the cool caress
of water – their bodies chalices,
raised to toast the sun.

One woman's son is the other's lover.

The mother's body – wrenched – was his way in.
The lover's body – breached – his way out.

Through the torrent of years,
across the pool's disquiet:
the mother catches what she once was -
the lover glimpses what she might become.

Dive under; enter the stippled skin.

They dress, caress, and part;
the son – the lover –

oblivious

rides on astride their hearts.

Generation

I have delivered my children to their lives
with the hot tongs of my body.
They do not look back.
What lies ahead the only story.

I am a discarded lathe
– their shape is already made.
I have woken in the night
to an empty house,
my throat filled with sawdust.

Radiant, ignorant women
display their babies – small stories -
already wandering away.

This painful blade forms me:
I am turned, returned,
shaping sharp as
pencil.

Miracle

I wished for miracles when I was young
– like Thomas, who saw the stabbed
hands of Jesus, and slid his fingers
right inside His wounded heart.

There was the miracle of a man
who loved and wished to marry me;
yet, from another angle, this was
unremarkable. The inconceivable miracle

of our children – their lives arriving
out of mine – was also, strangely, ordinary.
The sacrament of marriage - which I had taken
to be flesh and blood - converted miraculously

back to paper, and, with surprising ease,
was lost. Then the nails, thorns, the long
strung stay; waiting for the ever-hopeful flesh
finally to surrender. A burial behind stone -

these things are commonplace. The year
of the third infidelity, third time denied,
my heart and sex stabbed, all that's sacred
butchered, knived – the last day of that year,

it was still, and cloudless. I needed a tempest
to rage and scourge the pain, debride my hurt,
and with rain to re-annoint me. I might, even,
have prayed. That night, unseasonably,

light cracked the sky's slate, and thunder rolled
the stone aside. Hot spats pattered; then water
drummed its fingers down upon the house.
I was re-made that night – composed

within the tender power of miracle.
Before the brave new year unsheathed its blade
in order to dispatch that which could no longer
serve, I went to urinate, and found that I had bled.

The Difficult Gift

Here again: the difficult gift of love arrives
– a parcel placed in my hands.
The sensible thing is to refuse, knowing
it isn't possible to live with certain gifts.

A parcel arrives, placed in my hands.
And I accept, trying this time to learn
how the gift might possibly be lived with.
After all, this pain is not the same as love.

I must accept it, try to understand
the motive and invention of the giver.
After all this pain, I can't correctly see love –
the trout that breathes polluted water.

The motive and invention of the giver
test the filters I have put in place.
A trout might die in these polluted waters.
How to keep myself and be true to love?

The filters I have put in place test
what to admit, what to refuse.
How might I be myself, and be true
to this difficult guest, arriving, bearing gifts?

Other poetry titles by Modjaji Books

Fourth Child
by Megan Hall

Life in Translation
by Azila Talit Reisenberger

Burnt Offering
by Joan Metelerkamp

Oleander
by Fiona Zerbst

Strange Fruit
by Helen Moffett

Please, Take Photographs
by Sindiwe Magona

removing
by Melissa Butler

Missing
by Beverly Rycroft

These are the Lies I told you
by Kerry Hammerton

The Suitable Girl
by Michelle McGrane

Conduit
by Sarah Frost

modjaji books

http://modjaji.book.co.za